T0354990

INTROVERT LEADERS
STOP HIDING
THE WORLD NEEDS YOU

INTROVERT LEADERS
STOP HIDING
THE WORLD NEEDS YOU

ROBERT F. LOWERY

INTROVERT LEADERS STOP HIDING
THE WORLD NEEDS YOU

iUniverse books may be ordered through booksellers or by contacting:

iUniverse
1663 Liberty Drive
Bloomington, IN 47403
www.iuniverse.com
844-349-9409

ISBN: 978-1-6632-6306-3 (sc)
ISBN: 978-1-6632-6305-6 (e)

Library of Congress Control Number: 2024909969

Print information available on the last page.

iUniverse rev. date: 05/22/2024

CONTENTS

CHAPTER 1

INTROVERTS, STOP CONFORMING

I always wanted to pursue a job or career where I could stay behind the scenes—a job where I was solely responsible for myself and identified by an employee number. It appears God wanted something different.

I didn't become aware of my social anxiety and occasional awkwardness until I dove deeper into my self-development journey. Being labeled "quiet" and "shy" bothered me so much that there were times when I thought if I attended more leadership training or public speaking classes, I could get rid of those labels and become more outspoken, with skill sets matching extrovert leaders.

Unsurprisingly, I failed terribly at trying to be like others. I hated that I couldn't perform well at networking events with large groups. The fact that I couldn't make myself the loudest person in the room only confirmed that I couldn't become an effective leader—but I didn't let that false belief discourage me from trying to improve inwardly so that I could be better outwardly.

I believe wholeheartedly in self-development. It's a continuous process of unraveling the layers of who you are and understanding your beliefs, values, traumas, habits, desires, needs, and wants. To be the best version of yourself, you must actively learn and grow in these areas.

My self-development journey started with God. I don't mean religion but God. Seeking God and God alone allowed me to develop the most intimate relationship I will ever experience. Through my flaws, mistakes, and insecurities, God helped me discover my purpose. And when walking in my purpose, God showed me how uniquely and wonderfully I was made.

I stopped trying to be like other extroverted leaders and tapped into the unique gifts God had given me as an *introvert* leader. I no longer have to be the loudest in the room or the most charismatic. Instead, I'm wired to be purpose-driven and fixated on empowering others to see their own potential. As an introvert leader, I need purpose behind everything I do. Once I lock into that purpose, I find the strength to overcome any fears or doubts.

Because of my self-development journey with God, I've now had the privilege to lead a department of over 100 people, facilitate training sessions across the U.S., serve on boards and committees in various leadership capacities, publicly speak at numerous events, build my own business, mentor and coach others, and start a podcast. The greatest part is that I achieved all this in my own way—by being me, an introvert leader.

CHAPTER 2

WHO IS AND ISN'T AN INTROVERT LEADER?

I won't say that everyone is an introvert leader because not everyone is an introvert or a leader. Some people are one of them, but not both. Others think they're both when they're neither. Knowing whether you're an introvert leader starts with understanding who you are at your core. I learned I was an introvert leader after discovering more about myself. Without knowing who I was, I couldn't possibly know who God created me to be.

If you're just beginning your self-development journey or need to dive deeper to know what makes you uniquely you, don't skip ahead in this eBook and try to learn if you're an introvert leader. First, answer these self-reflection questions to reveal the undiscovered parts of yourself:

1. What are your top three values?
2. What are five words that describe you?
3. How do you like to recharge?
4. What do you enjoy doing in your free time?
5. How do you add value to others?
6. What motivates you?
7. What are your top 3-5 skills?
8. What are your top 3-5 natural talents?

Do you have the answers to these questions? If so, you can start diving into what an introvert is and what a leader is. From there, you can determine whether you match the definition and qualities of an introvert, leader, and introvert leader.

What is an Introvert?

An introvert is a person who prefers retreating to and focusing on their inner thoughts versus external stimuli. They like spending time with small groups versus crowds. But despite popular belief, not all introverts are quiet, shy loners. They simply process the world differently than extroverts.

In 1920, psychologist Carl Jung started using the terms "introvert" and "extrovert." One of the ways Jung differentiated the two was how they got energy. According to Jung, introverts turn inward to their own thoughts to relax and recharge, while extroverts turn to others.

Nearly one-third to one-half of all people in the U.S. identify as introverts, although introversion can look slightly different, depending on the person. Generally, though, several patterns signal whether you're an introvert. You may be this personality type if you agree with most of the following:

- Prefer to work alone versus doing group work
- Enjoy and feel comfortable being alone
- Like to spend time reflecting
- Are self-aware

- Mull over information before making decisions
- Concentrate best in quiet environments
- Retreat to your inner thoughts to rest
- Feel tired after being in big groups or crowds
- Daydream often
- Have few but very close friendships
- Use your imagination to solve problems
- Prefer to write than talk

Don't worry if you can't see all of these qualities in yourself. There are four different types of introverts, so you may align with specific attributes more than others. For context, here are the various types of introverts.

1. Social Introvert

A social introvert will gravitate towards a small group versus a crowd or large group. They don't need a night out to have fun. This type of introvert prefers a quiet night alone in their home or with a few close friends or family.

2. Thinking Introvert

An introvert in this category will be very introspective. They'll spend a significant amount of time thinking, enabling them to be more creative.

3. Anxious Introvert

This type of introvert usually feels nervous or unsettled around people, particularly during social interactions. They often overthink the potential outcome of an interaction, which typically prevents them from conversing and engaging with others.

4. Inhibited Introvert

An inhibited introvert won't make a decision before contemplating it from every angle. They spend a lot of time considering what to do before they make a move.

Confirmation is Key

If you're unsure whether you're an introvert or what type of introvert you are (you could be a specific one or a mixture of multiple), seek confirmation. Even if you're confident in your decision, verify it. You can do this in two ways.

First, you can ask people you trust for feedback. Close family members or friends will have unique insights and perspectives based on their experiences and interactions with you.

Secondly, you can take an online personality test. There are many available, like the Myers-Briggs Type Indicator and Enneagram Personality Test. Both have pros and cons, but they will still provide a better idea of whether you're an introvert.

What is a Leader?

Now that you know what it means to be an introvert, it's time to explore what it means to be a leader. In simple terms, a leader will be at least one of the following:

- Inspirational and motivating
- A visionary who articulates a path to success
- Supportive and quick to provide helpful tools to their teams
- Empowering and great at building up other leaders

Checking one of these boxes is essential to being a leader, but checking all of them is required to be a great one. The best leaders know how to **inspire** and **motivate** their teams to achieve a **vision** and will not only equip their followers with a **path** to **success** but also with **tools** and **empowerment** to ensure they accomplish the goal and become leaders along the way. It doesn't matter if the team's route is long or short, hard or simple, or slow or fast-paced. Effective leaders will guide their teams to success the entire way. That's because they typically do ten key things almost every day:

1. Sharpen Their Expertise

No one likes to follow someone who doesn't know what they're doing, which is why good leaders are always sharpening their skill set. They're never content with mediocrity or staying the same. Exceptional leaders are always developing, growing, and expanding their talents.

2. Articulate Their Vision

God said without a vision, the people perish.

Effective leaders keep their vision top of mind and repeat it to their teams to keep everyone invested and mindful of why they're working towards their goal. It's easy to forget the "why" in the day-to-day grind, but a good leader won't let it happen too easily.

3. Set Priorities

Great leaders know all too well that focusing on everything means you're not focusing on anything. A successful leader will make priorities clear and encourage everyone to focus on the main agenda to ensure their team progresses and doesn't get distracted by the little things.

4. Provide Details

Leading means giving information to people who need it the most: the ones accomplishing the goal. Effective leaders don't withhold valuable information from their teams. They're transparent and quick to provide whatever insights people need to realize the vision ahead.

5. Make Decisions

Successful leaders are decisive. They don't overthink. They don't rack their brains looking for the right answer. They work with what they have—including available information and their expertise—to make the best decisions possible to aid their teams.

6. Show Empathy

Great leaders view things from others' perspectives and try to see things differently. That doesn't mean they're pushovers. But it does mean they care enough about their teams to seek understanding and pivot if necessary.

7. Encourage Teamwork

We all know there's no "I" in team—but effective leaders don't just know it. They live by it. Successful leaders don't do everything by themselves, and they don't ask their team members to do so, either. Instead, they recognize everyone's unique gifts and talents and encourage teamwork and collaboration, knowing it produces better results.

8. Hold Themselves Accountable

You won't find an effective leader placing blame on someone else. Those who are the best at leading teams will take accountability for their mistakes, whether they're intentional or not. And if the team ever misses the mark, a great leader will accept collective blame before encouraging everyone to keep moving forward.

9. Communicate Clearly

There's no confusion when speaking to a great leader. They're effective communicators. They don't backpedal, mumble, or shake when they're speaking. Instead, they're confident in their words. They explain their message clearly, and they back up what they say.

10. Praise and Celebrate Others

When someone hits a goal, goes the extra mile, or is simply consistent in what they do, successful leaders acknowledge them. They praise and celebrate their team members' wins, reliability, and milestones.

11. Create More Leaders

Great leaders don't want to be the only leaders. They want to build other leaders as well. They want to share the responsibility of guiding and inspiring a team, and they aren't threatened by the prospect of others coming alongside to help them.

Assess Your Leadership Qualities

Knowing whether you're a leader is hard, especially if you've never been in a leadership position. But just like with personality tests, you can get the insight you need by taking an online leadership test. There are tons to choose from—however, make sure you answer the test questions honestly. Assess yourself with eyes wide open, not through the lens of *wanting* to be a leader.

The goal is to know who you are right now. And even if you're not a leader today, you may be one in the future, so don't get discouraged by the results. For the purposes of this eBook, the outcome of any leadership test is only helping you determine whether you're an introvert leader so that you know how to be a great one.

What is an Introvert Leader?

Once you're confident you're an introvert and a leader, you can combine the two terms to call yourself an introvert leader. This type of person is someone who's aware and embraces their inner strengths and qualities in order to influence others to a common vision or goal.

If you're afraid of embracing this leadership style because you think you'll be the oddball looking in, please know that won't be the case. You and I aren't the only introvert leaders. Karl Moore, a professor and researcher at McGill University in Canada, conducted a study and found that out of 400 CEOs, about one-third of them identified as introverts. Among middle and first-line managers, the percentage of introverts was even higher.

All that to say—welcome to the club.

CHAPTER 3

MYTHS AND BENEFITS OF BEING AN INTROVERT LEADER

From one introvert leader to another, you should know this title comes with some myths. In fact, you might be thinking of one right now, and I wouldn't blame you. In the past, I never understood how "introvert" and "leader" could fit side-by-side to become a title I was proud to wear. But let me tell you from experience, fellow introvert leader: what you think you know may be incorrect.

There are three common beliefs about introvert leaders, and I'm here to tell you why each one of them is a myth.

Myth #1: Introvert Leaders Lack People Skills

Believe me when I say this: people skills do not equate to being the loudest person in the room or having charisma and charm. Don't believe it? A study published in Harvard Business Review proves it.

After researchers reviewed a database of 17,000 executives, they found that charismatic people were more than twice as likely to be hired as CEOs. However, charisma didn't mean they performed well once hired.

Researchers discovered that introvert leaders actually exceeded expectations in the workplace. While they weren't as bubbly as extroverted leaders, they picked up on emotional cues and sensory details. Their frontal lobes and thalamus—two parts of the brain that deal with problem-solving and internal processing— also received more blood flow than extroverts. Researchers believe this boost gave introvert leaders a better chance at handling personal or complex situations on small teams.

Myth 2: Introvert Leaders Are Poor Communicators

Among the many events I've gone to, I'm sure someone somewhere mistook my internal processing for disinterest—even though it couldn't be further from the truth. I'm engaged at every event I attend, whether I'm speaking, sitting, or networking. But I'm a methodical thinker and an active listener.

As an introvert, I internally consider various scenarios, outcomes, and factors, and I listen to others before I speak. That doesn't make me a bad communicator, and it doesn't make you one, either. In fact, it makes you a better communicator because you don't voice every unfiltered thought, potentially producing confusion or misguidance on your team. It also means you don't rush to speak over others, preferring to gather insight and intel to make a well-articulated, calculated, and strategic point. That's a great leadership quality that's unique to introverts, and research proves it. A study found that introverts use more concrete, precise language when describing things.

Myth #3: Introvert Leaders Despise Group Work

I won't lie. Given the introverted nature of introvert leaders, working solo is the preference—but that doesn't mean it's the go-to option day in and day out. Introvert leaders know when collaboration is best and excel at working with others.

A study conducted by The Hustle found that 89% of introvert leaders enjoy professional collaboration. A study conducted by Harvard Business School also found that, while extroverts were great at leading passive teams, introverts were more effective at leading *proactive* teams. The reason? Introvert leaders weren't threatened by collaborative input. They welcomed and readily received suggestions and paid more attention to micro-expressions.

The skills an introvert leader brings to a collaborative environment even increase profitability and productivity. A study published in the Academy of Management Journal examined 57 managers and 374 employees across 30 branches of a pizza chain. The researchers found that introvert-led franchises were 20% more profitable than ones led by extroverts. They also conducted another study and discovered that when 163 students split into 56 groups and were given 10 minutes to fold as many t-shirts as possible, the teams led by introverts were up to 28% more productive than groups led by extroverts.

Natural Qualities of Introvert Leaders

Let's be honest—being an introvert leader is a superpower. It's not a burden or weakness. It's a strength. All you have to do is embrace it.

Stop mimicking extroverts. Stop trying to be the loudest. Stop trying to be the most talkative or charismatic person in the room. Leave that to the people who actually are those things; they're better at it than you. And that's not because you're less than them. It's simply because their personality type and leadership style are different from yours, and they've embraced their unique quirks and gifts. You must do the same if you want to be a successful introvert leader.

You have natural qualities that make you great. You are gifted in ways extrovert leaders aren't—and if you don't believe that, here's a list of unique, necessary natural qualities you possess as an introvert leader:

- Highly creative
- A problem-solving guru
- Relationship-oriented (allowing you to build deep, meaningful connections)
- Focused
- Present
- Connected to your environment
- Thoughtful
- A great listener
- Curious (this helps you ask great questions to get to the root of something)
- Adaptable

- Empathetic
- Purpose-driven
- Collaborative
- A smart risk-taker (because you consider things so carefully)

And the list can go on….

You have so much to offer the world by embracing your introvert leadership qualities. Some of the most impactful people of all time are introvert leaders.

Albert Einstein, Rosa Parks, Steven Spielberg, Bill Gates, Al Gore, JK Rowling, Warren Buffet, Mahatma Gandhi, Charles Darwin, Michael Jordan, Barack Obama, and Dr. Seuss are just *some* of the people who you can call introvert leaders. There are hundreds of more out there. So, will you confidently step into the rank of this leadership type?

CHAPTER 4

STEP INTO YOUR POWER

If you accept the call to embrace your nature as an introvert leader, you have to unlock the power of this part of your identity. Your purpose depends on it. Your future depends on it. Your satisfaction—the inner peace you have when embracing who you really are—also depends on it. You can't afford to reject your God-given leadership style, not unless you want to waste time.

So, how do you unlock your power as an introvert leader to make a positive impact on the world? There are five strategies you can implement.

1. Inspire Innovation With Your Observation and Listening Skills

Taking in and processing mountains of information, perspectives, problems, solutions, and opinions can be draining for some people. But for introvert leaders, it can be insightful and produce innovation.

Whenever you're leading, don't be afraid to gather as many team members as possible to collaborate and brainstorm about solutions to issues. In those settings, use your natural abilities to observe and listen to formulate game-winning ideas. You have an innate gift to mull things over before speaking or suggesting something insightful, so bring that gift to the table. Your ability to process scattered information and transform it into a creative solution will produce ideas no one is considering.

2. Let Your Results Speak for You

If verbal communication isn't your strong suit, don't be discouraged—you live in a world where actions speak louder than words. Results matter more than promises. You don't have to be the loudest person in the room when you exceed expectations on every deliverable you offer.

When people see you're credible, consistent, competent, and overall excellent at what you do, you don't need to use words to prove you're adding value. Your results will prove it for you, so focus on utilizing your creativity, problem-solving skills, thoughtfulness, concentration, and collaborative talents to produce work that speaks louder than words.

3. Schedule Alone Time to Recharge Your Energy Levels

No matter what, you'll need to speak to others regularly if you're a leader. This part of the job will naturally energize extroverts, allowing them to perform well—but that doesn't mean you, as an introvert leader, can't perform well, too. You simply need to schedule alone time in between meetings or events to rest and recharge. And you need to do it intentionally.

This step may require you to block out time on your calendar that literally says "Quiet Hours." That way, you (and everyone who should know) are fully aware when it's time for you to relax and recharge your energy levels. Introvert leaders often fail to present themselves well around others because they haven't taken adequate time to retreat to increase their energy. But with intentionality, introvert leaders can get the alone time they need to ensure they're energized enough to perform exceptionally during every interaction.

4. Prepare Talking Points to Ace Meetings

When you have a natural inkling to mull over information or a topic before speaking, you must get an agenda before a meeting starts. That way, you can take time to prepare talking points that will speak specifically to your audience and achieve the desired outcome of the meeting.

Planning ahead will give you room to creatively and critically think about the best points to mention, solidify your confidence going into the meeting, and relieve any self-imposed pressure to figure it all out on the spot. Of course, this tip may sound like a basic strategy to ace any presentation, but it's also crucial to being an effective introvert leader. After all, many introverts would rather write than talk, so jotting down your thoughts before a meeting will make talking during it more preferable and enjoyable.

5. Deepen Relationships With One-on-One Meeting

Introverts typically thrive in one-on-one interactions or among small groups, so if you're leading people, schedule these types of meetings whenever possible. In these settings, your listening skills, empathy, thoughtfulness, curiosity, and observant nature will produce thought-provoking questions and deep conversations, all of which will help you strengthen relationships with team members and solve complex problems.

The people following you will enjoy your unique insights and acute ability to relate and show genuine care. They will be more engaged and productive when they know their leader doesn't just dole out tasks but also seeks to help, inspire, and know them on a personal level.

Build the Foundation

The strategies in this eBook aren't the only ones you need to step into your power as an introvert leader, but they are the foundation. They're the floor you need to stand on before taking additional steps to unlock the power of this leadership style. So, practice and master implementing these strategies. Then, check your results after three months. If you've used these tips consistently and have produced good results—which you should—you can start brainstorming your own ways to unleash your power as an introvert leader.

You're a highly creative thinker and a visionary. It's part of your nature as an introvert leader. You don't need this eBook to give you all the answers. You simply need it to build a foundation. Once that foundation is set and you're operating confidently, you'll have the footing to take more steps to unlock deeper levels of success that come with being an introvert leader.

CHAPTER 5

THE CALL TO INTROVERT LEADERSHIP

The world is waiting for you. It's not waiting for the extroverted side of you that you're trying to force into existence. People are waiting for the authentic, unique parts of you to come out of hiding.

The world needs more confident introvert leaders. It needs more executives and managers who are slow to speak, quick to listen, highly creative, empathetic, collaborative, deeply relational, purpose-driven, methodical, and eager to build up other leaders. In a world where 76% of job seekers say their boss is toxic, workplaces will benefit from the natural gifts you possess as an introvert leader. Even sports teams and classrooms will see greater success and harmony.

So don't hide, and don't pretend to be something you're not. You are who you are for a reason. Embrace it and watch those around you change. Your unapologetic commitment to being you, an introvert leader, will be just the thing that builds better teams and interactions worldwide.

RESOURCES

1. Rachel Reiff Ellis. Introvert Personality. WebMD. https://www.webmd.com/balance/introvert-personality-overview

2. Shonna Waters, PhD. What is a leader, what do they do, and how do you become one? BetterUp. https://www.betterup.com/blog/what-is-a-leader-and-how-do-you-become-one

3. Bill Murphy Jr. 20 Signs You're Working With a True Leader—and Not Just a Boss. The Muse. https://www.themuse.com/advice/20-signs-youre-working-with-a-true-leaderand-not-just-a-boss

4. Introvert Leadership: Tips for Managing Introverts (or being an Introverted Leader yourself). Management 3.0. https://management30.com/blog/introvert-leadership/

5. Jena McGregor. Introverts tend to be better CEOs — and other surprising traits of top-performing executives. Washington Post. https://www.washingtonpost.com/news/on-leadership/wp/2017/04/17/introverts-tend-to-be-better-ceos-and-other-surprising-traits-of-top-performing-executives/

6. D L Johnson, J S Wiebe, S M Gold, N C Andreasen, R D Hichwa, G L Watkins, L L Boles Ponto. Cerebral blood flow and personality: a positron emission tomography study. National Library of Medicine. https://pubmed.ncbi.nlm.nih.gov/9989562/

7. Happiness Found With Introversion: 10 Psychological Research Studies. Psych2Go. https://psych2go.net/happiness-found-with-introversion-10-psychological-research-studies/

8. Zachary Crockett. 65% of execs think introverts are bad leaders. Here's why that's BS. The Hustle. https://thehustle.co/65-of-execs-think-introverts-are-bad-leaders-heres-why-thats-bs/

9. Carmen Nobel. Introverts: The Best Leaders for Proactive Employees. Harvard Business School. https://hbswk.hbs.edu/item/introverts-the-best-leaders-for-proactive-employees

10. Candace Atamanik. The Introverted Leader: Examining the Role of Personality and Environment. Florida International University FIU Digital Commons. Center for Leadership Current Research. College of Arts, Science, and Education. https://digitalcommons.fiu.edu/cgi/viewcontent.cgi?referer=&httpsredir=1&article=1001&context=lead_research

11. Adam M. Grant, Francesca Gino, David A. Hofmann. Reversing the Extraverted Leadership Advantage: The Role of Employee Productivity. Academy of Management Journal. https://static1.squarespace.com/static/55dcde36e4b0df55a96ab220/t/55e5f374e4b04539eab51172/1441133428448/GrantGinoHofmann_Reversing.pdf

12. John Rampton. 23 of the Most Amazingly Successful Introverts in History. Inc. https://www.inc.com/john-rampton/23-amazingly-successful-introverts-throughout-history.html

13. Gene Marks. Monster Poll: 76 Percent of Job Seekers Say Their Boss is 'Toxic.' Inc. https://www.inc.com/gene-marks/monster-poll-76-percent-of-job-seekers-say-their-boss-is-toxic.html

Printed in the United States
by Baker & Taylor Publisher Services